Socorro

Socorro

Poems of New Mexico

Tony Reevy

Iris Press
Oak Ridge, Tennessee

Copyright © 2017 by Tony Reevy

All rights reserved. No portion of this book may be reproduced in any form or by any means, including electronic storage and retrieval systems, without explicit, prior written permission of the publisher, except for brief passages excerpted for review and critical purposes.

Cover Photo:
Llano de San Juan, New Mexico, Catholic Church.
1940. Russell Lee.
Library of Congress, Prints & Photographs Division,
FSA-OWI Collection, LC-USF35-376

Cover Background Texture:
handmade paper by Suzanne Brown

Book Design:
Robert B. Cumming, Jr.

Library of Congress Cataloging-in-Publication Data

Names: Reevy, Tony, author.
Title: Socorro : poems of New Mexico / Tony Reevy.
Description: Oak Ridge, Tennessee : Iris Press, [2017]
Identifiers: LCCN 2017001605 | ISBN 9781604542448 (pbk. : alk. paper)
Subjects: LCSH: New Mexico—Poetry.
Classification: LCC PS3618.E4459 S63 2017 | DDC 811/.6—dc23
LC record available at https://lccn.loc.gov/2017001605

Acknowledgments

Many of these poems first appeared in the chapbooks *Green Cove Stop* (Finishing Line Press, 2002), *Magdalena* (Pudding House Publications, 2004), *Lightning in Wartime* (Finishing Line Press, 2007), and *In Mountain Lion Country* (Pudding House Publications, 2009). *In Mountain Lion Country* is composed entirely of poems about New Mexico, and *Magdalena* contains a sequence of poems about New Mexico. The author would also like to acknowledge the following publications where some of these poems first appeared: "The Chief", *Asheville Poetry Review*; "Minor Accident, End of Term, Spring 1970" in Joseph Zaccardi, editor, *Changing Harm to Harmony: Bullies and Bystanders* (Marin Poetry Center Press, 2015); "Mrs. Carty", *Levelerpoetry.com*; "The Ice Boy's Mother", *Naugatuck Review*; "Miracle", *Oracle*; "Prophecy" in Timothy F. Crowley, editor, *Poets for Peace: A Collection* (The Chapel Hill Press, Inc., 2002); "All Saints, All Souls", *R-KV-RY*; "In Mountain Lion Country", "Stalking *Asparagus officinalis*, Socorro, New Mexico, 1970," *Terrain.org*; "Second Grade, Zimmerly School", *The Blotter Magazine*; "Seeking Jewels", *The Whirlwind Review*; "Dreaming of Luminarias at Noche Buena", *Windhover*.

First, with many thanks to my family—Caroline, Lindley and Ian—for their patience and support, and with thanks to my poetry group, Bruce, Kathy, Korki, Priscilla, and Renata, who reviewed many of these poems. Finally, many thanks to Bob Cumming and Beto Cumming at Iris Press for their continuing support for my work.

Contents

I: Childhood

Child of the Desert • 15
Town Near the Trinity Site • 16
Magdalena • 17
Ghost Town Bank (Kelly, New Mexico) • 18
Old Town • 19
All Saints, All Souls • 20
Dreaming of Luminarias at Noche Buena • 21
In Mountain Lion Country • 22
Will-o'-the-Wisp • 24
Forty-Niner's Day • 25
Abandoned Mine • 26
Beautiful Lake • 27
Second Grade, Zimmerly School • 28
Abandoned Motorcycle in Adobe Wall Corner • 29
The Curandera • 30
The Captain's Clubhouse • 31
Panning After a Storm • 32
The Green Ghost • 33
Kelly Mine • 34
Mrs. Carty • 35
Stalking *Asparagus officinalis,* Socorro, New Mexico, 1970 • 36
Minor Accident, End of Term, Spring 1970 • 38
Facilities Storage Lot, Socorro, New Mexico, 1970 • 39
Ghost • 40
Recess • 41
Bottle Collectors • 42
Dream of Valverde Field • 43
Field Trip, December 1971 • 44
First Week in Troy—1972 • 45
Elegy—Sarah and Freddie the Freeloader • 46

II: Legends

Elfego Baca • 51
Blood-Heart Moon • 52

The Treasure of San Miguel • 53
San Marcial • 54
Flash Flood • 55
The Magdalene • 56
Railroad Corral, Magdalena • 57
Miracle at Laguna • 58
San Juan Church • 59
The Parley with General Sherman, Bosque Redondo • 60
Captain Mills' Decision • 61
Lamy • 62
Zozobra (Old Man Gloom) • 63
From the Cordova Church • 64
Bulto of San Francisco de Asis • 65
The Place of the Fiddle • 66
The Ice Boy's Mother • 67
Ranchos de Taos, Noon • 68
The Death of Fray Ramírez • 69
La Llorona of Manuelito • 70

III: Dreaming

By the Palace of the Governors • 73
Miracle • 74
The Chief • 75
To Rudolfo Anaya • 77
San Esteban del Rey • 78
Seeking Jewels • 79
Zuni Event Day • 80
Stickmen at Chaco • 81
Playtime • 82
Prophecy • 83

Glossary • 87
Notes • 93

In memory of
Bill Reevy (Stefan Révay),
1922-2017

I: Childhood

Child of the Desert

Little boy, do not step
unshod. The desert is not
as it seems. These dry vines
have goatheads to prick
your feet. Centipedes
mill the path, and snakes
warm there by night.

But shoes hold danger, so
shake out the scorpions.
The ugliest vermin, though—
child of the desert,
vinegarroon: squat, menacing
in the porch light—
is harmless.

Coyotes or a blizzard
took your cat. The new one
kills rattlers in the back
yard. Lights dance over
the mountains; summer
storms drift in before sun
falls, leavening the air
with sage.

Town Near the Trinity Site

Christmas Eve.
Dusty desert town
dotted by candle-lit
luminarias. Pinyon balms
chill winter air.

Warm glow from
windows. People walk
house to house.
This is Nuevo México,
this is the new world.

In the adobes—
the Bacas', the Chavezes'—
biscochitos, toddies,
spice scent of cider,
tang of aged wood.

The plaza—rare trees,
bandstand—ringed
by lights. Silent.
No houses. No one
to visit here.

On a pedestal by the
stand—marked with
a plaque—a black, pitted
shell. Part of
the first crater.

He is born,
he is born.
It was
born here.

Magdalena

Water tanks,
windmills,
brown-lump cattle.

This was
the wild land.

Railhead,
stockyard,
looming mine
tipple.

The stores,
smelling of old
boots and
Wonder Bread.

The beeves are sparse,
sage and prickly
pear crowd
in.

Ranked mountains,
dotted by green
pinyon, box up
the desert.

Some days, even the
West
is small.

Ghost Town Bank (Kelly, New Mexico)

Pinyon scent over
grit-dusted rock,
foundation stones,
rotted wood.

In the corner,
sunk to dirt, a
safe. Door hangs
open loosely,

sides rust, flake.
Show inner and
outer steel plates,
concrete-filled,

bullet-riddled.
Slugs passed
through; glanced
off, dishing the sides;

lodged in the
walls—white-weathered
lead dollops, like
dried lumps of clay.

The safe set here
forever, or at least
until it rusts
and crumbles.

One thing
scavengers, antique
hunters, prospectors
can't haul away.

Old Town

There is a place
with cedar awning posts polished
by generations of visitors' hands,

shops scented by pinyon incense,
   potpourri,

where after-dinner dusk walkers must
step aside for ghost-tour groups
and the plaza's too crowded.

But San Felipé de Neri still towers
over all.

And, in late-night calm—adobe-lined alleys,
empty sidewalks, silent shops. Crowds
vanished, tour-guide lanterns dark.

Tang of dust, of Rio Grande water
from nearby valley—

Then, don't be afraid
to love this tourist-haunted place
for what
  it
      is.

All Saints, All Souls

Saints are hallowed,
but so are the souls,
and the least ones,
wills-o'-the-wisp,
ranged down the
street, glimmering caramel-
orange, greeting bat-
winged, caped walkers
of the night—all searching
to fill an emptiness
they carry with them.

At full light,
a mother counts her
lost ones, remembers
one, puts a taper
to the candle for her
little girl, wandering,
 a dancing flame,
  all that day
   and more.

Dreaming of Luminarias at Noche Buena[1]

Paper-caged light
from candles etching
plumb lines of buildings,

occasional flicker flare burn
as wind blows bag
against flame—courtyard, orange

bonfire torching, chimneys,
woodstove flues, fume
of pinyon, San Miguel's

tolls ending Misa,
people drifting home
—boy breaks

from family,
looks in establo
to see animals kneel,

greet the Lord
with rare, soon-vanished gift
of God's Word.

In Mountain Lion Country

Winter meant pinyon nuts.

The drive on highway
60, up from Rio Grande
to the peaks,

ruined smelter, rusted
branch line falling away
as our station wagon
climbs.

Then, rutted road to the
ghost town—hardly a
shed, much less a house.

Just above, shrubby
green trees:

pinyon pines.

In their cones, the
brown nuts.

I stumble, my
tiny sisters toddle.

We shake the nuts
into bags, dreaming of
biscochitos, Posadas,
the Christmas tree.

Mom and Dad watch.

Snakes are denned
for the season, but

cougars stir
in the hills,

the rusty tipple
rattles,

the mine tunnel
gapes.

Better to stay with
the pinyons.

Leave tailings, wire
ropes, shafts
to the miners

whose bones
lie in town
or below.

Will-o'-the-Wisp[2]

Lights flicker
above the mountain,
children sit on the carport
and watch.

The town below
is small, quiet.

A train, blue and yellow,
snakes the Rio
Grande, whistles
for Manzanares Street.

One of the kids,
a boy, takes a photo
with the old Brownie.

White spots in western
sky—camera defect, extra-
terrestrial, government test—

prints are brittle now,
preserving a view
freighted with dreams.

Forty-Niner's Day[3]

The boy disappeared
in a sea
of green muck—

on Forty-Niner's Day
also St. Paddy's Day
in a desert town—

then broke the surface
with his head,
a green-spattered seal.

This—and a sea
of beer bottles—
is how we celebrate

when women are few,
the closest city
an hour's drive.

Nightfall—coyotes
approach the abandoned
pit, sniff at

mixed shaving cream
and beer; stop short
and back away.

Abandoned Mine

Life's like that.
Dad rolled his words
slow, quiet.
We were looking down.

In the tunnel's
hard black,
the flashlight threw
a feeble cone.

The cougar tracks,
just spotted,
went in but
didn't come out.

Beautiful Lake

From Bonita at sundown
into the pan, with
bacon, but first I
traced the trout on
Dad's shirt cardboard
in magic marker. Thirteen
inches, was it? Not
bad for that lake.
Taken on bait—Dad
had flies, but
grew up on a farm,
liked a coffee can
full of grounds
crawling with worms.

At night, the camp
was silent, except one
time, when a shuffling
nomad passed our
tent, tipped the trash
can. Dad shook me
at dawn—*Did you
hear it, did you hear
it?* he hissed. Bear
could have ripped our
tent like a paper towel.
No, safe in a dream of
childhood, warm, I
had slept on.

Second Grade, Zimmerly School

The hands on the classroom
clock advanced
with a soundless sweep.

Cursive letters loomed,
white on green, on a strip
above the blackboard
as I labored, pencil-scratching
in my *Printing Power* workbook.

But what I liked to watch in class
was Mrs. Grice—my teacher—
young, quick, pretty.
Her arm swept white lines
across the blackboard.

Then, her perfume followed
when she leaned over me,
guiding my hand
with her hand
as she taught me
to write.

Abandoned Motorcycle in Adobe Wall Corner

Recalled the English
soldier in a movie
riding, wearing goggles,
about to crash.

With a second-grade
girlfriend in back, I
played on that cycle,
pretended to ride.

Like the men we'd
both seen on the new
Interstate, with women
behind them, slashing

the Jornada del Muerto
from Socorro to
Albuquerque. Took
a part or two off—

then Celestina's father
yelled at me, *Leading
his daughter wrong.
That hog must belong

to someone.* Returned
to a yard filled with
artifacts we'd trucked
home from abandoned

mines in our '65
Fairlane station wagon.
Felt confused, then re-
assured, then justified.

The Curandera

Some of the yerbas she finds
at the Rexall by the plaza,
but osha, blue corn, others come
from field, plain, arroyo, mountain.

The owl called outside Baca's window
three nights now, and the ball
in his stomach grows
with the waxing moon.

The water boils in the pot, the boy
asks if he can add the osha
to make the tea. She says no—
it only lives in her hand.

He will learn, maybe, or not—
as God wills.

The Captain's Clubhouse[4]

Captain Billy shot
in the station lobby.
By an angry man,
the man's wife crying
in their car. The station
reported Billy's condition
hourly, daily. He held
on for weeks.

We kids prayed for him.
He'd have lived today,
but this was forty
years back. The trauma
was too much. The Captain
slipped into a coma,
never woke up.

Our hopes dashed, we
watched the TV memorial,
the Captain's hat, big,
fake moustache,
laid out before us
on our screens.

Panning After a Storm

When clouds pass, sage-scented
air. Water rush is gone.

In the arroyo, streaks of black
sand—scooped, panned, the gold

flakes revealed. Carefully sifted
into an old prescription bottle.

Wealth in plain sight—the arroyo
clefts the desert, as Magdalena

Mountains loom silent, pinyon-
dotted, in view past its end.

The Green Ghost

The boys fly kites
over the arroyo,
mountains in a still
line like giants behind,
the brave river before
them. As the daily blue-
yellow train passes,
the green ghost looms—

That night, a boy tries
to sleep,
but the phantom
rises again
in his near-dreams.

His mother tells him
it comes from a book
but, as a coyote
howls, it seems
that anything
can happen.

Kelly Mine

The shaft opened
in square center
of the tunnel. We

filed around, one-
by-one, on either
side. Our pack

leader, a mining
man, told us boys
to listen. It was

seconds before the
pebble splashed.
That night, I

dreamed a fall
into cold
water, absolute

black. The end—
no miracle, no way
out of freezing

murk and sheer,
slick walls. And
now the dream

comes back and
I hear the mine's
ghost tapping,

tapping on quartz
where the rock
fall caught him.

Mrs. Carty

Old bottles purpled
in sun perch
on the back porch shelf.

She talks of hunting
them in trash pits
near their homestead.

Family headed west,
eighteen-eighties,
grandfather settled

to work the lead-
zinc smelter, hands
trembling, lungs shot.

Husband built her this house
just before Hoover—
they held on.

She's not leaving.

Crow calls from the backyard,
sun slants through old flasks—
brown, green, claret, clear.

It's July, rainy season—
a thunderhead rises
over the mountain.

Stalking *Asparagus officinalis*, Socorro, New Mexico, 1970

Below the station,
picking wild asparagus.
The spears are
thin, just pale green.
There's a creosote
smell from the tracks.

The loud voice behind
us is rushing water
in the irrigation canal.
It grinds up kids, Mom
says, and spits them out
downstream.

The Rio Grande beyond
is barren, a great
sand box, play-
ground of snakes and
coyotes. But Hatch
has its chiles

and the brown water
runs through acequias,
under roads, into
backyard gardens in
town. That and the
sun brings melons,
corn, squash, peppers
green and red.

In my dreams, the
backyard gardens
still grow, the burros
are corralled along
dirt alleys in town, and
the river runs full.

But the asparagus—
straight, short,
succulent shoots,
unpicked, goes to
dimmed, woody seed.

Minor Accident, End of Term, Spring 1970

Dorm-porch college boys,
third-rate mech-tech school,
laughing at the kid
who lost it down the hill,
smashed bike, head over curb
into a wind-break tree.

Not one comes down to help.
Kid grips shattered bike,
drags it back home.

River of blood coursing down
the kid's t-shirt, a growing red
flower, flag of the sixties,
summer of love
and all that—

Wouldn't come out in the wash,
so the kid's mom throws
it in the trash can downstairs.

Facilities Storage Lot, Socorro, New Mexico, 1970

Sun is low in sky,
then fades. Hot metal—
old Army deuce and a half—
cools a bit.

The day's animals rest,
night-dwellers rise
to eat. A lizard warms
on the truck fender,
then scuttles
to survive the night.

Cast-offs of the jungle
war machine
are cheaply bought.

Ghost[5]

Dust-land haunted
with white dreams
must be the home
of ghosts.

In nightmares they come—
reaching for little ones
on the edge of waking—

as the pellucid woman walks
the WPA sidewalk
by the middle school,
chest-bullet blood welling.

Searching for her man
long moldered down to dust
in the mine.

Over years gone, her flesh
has fallen to strips.

She vanishes at dawn,
just before
the children come.

Recess

At recess, we'd
cross Garfield
to the Bacas'
store. There was
penny candy, sodas,
pea shooters. Dos
zotz, por favor,
three cents. Old
Baca, toothless,
silent, my teacher's
cousin, clasped
pennies at the
register. Boys—
I see them now
as Anglo or Hispano—
crowded in, Baca's
daughter watching.
Then, we'd stand
on the sidewalk
marked *WPA
1935*, bolt the
candy, hurry
back. Being late
meant a visit
with Mr. Garcia
and his paddle.

Last time home,
Garfield still a
school, but the
store a thrift
shop. Wonder if
the Bacas still
own it?

Bottle Collectors

Jagged glass chards,
opaqued and colored
by sun, rain,
now dug, cleaned and
boxed, seemed endless
at Fort Craig.

Where soldiers got
drunk on hospital
bitters, or fought
pneumonia, gangrene
with whiskey and
patent medicine.

Leaving this hoard,
some broken by
professional hunters
with a backhoe,
others by troopers
a hundred years gone.

The wind sweeps
dust, brings a taste
of water from the Rio
Grande, eases past
and then across the
Jornada del Muerto.

Dream of Valverde Field

Devil rider,
hooves grating
whiskey shards,
uniform scraps,
men's bones.

Holding the foot
of the Mesa de
la Contadera.

Desert night,
diablo, I
will not keep,
will not pass,
will not try again.

Field Trip, December 1971

The two-and-a-half ton
roared us up U. S. Sixty,
destination Cibola Forest,
to cut trees for a Cub
Scout Christmas sale.

I had a keyhole saw,
no gloves, managed to
fell one pinyon. The
driver, a pack dad,
helped drag it in.

He bought us chile and
pie in Datil, spoke not
a word about my
ineptness, my bad showing
against a pledge of
"Be Prepared."

That night, I dreamt
myself back to silent,
scented pines, to where
the moon shone
white as cut glass
through Noche
Buena air.

First Week in Troy—1972

A cold wind blows
down the Hudson
(this is before the
fish came back).

Fords and Chevys crawl up
the ice-slick avenue
canyoned by a
beetling shirt factory.

A boy, face pressed
against family-car window,
dreams warm bleakness
of the desert.

Moving, always moving.
Moving on, moving forward, moving
to and fro across a continent
as if the meanest peninsula.

This is America. This is the
covered wagon, lightning
express, clipper ship
in the modern world.

This is a boy, face against
the safety glass,
wishing he had a,
wishing he knew where was,
home.

Elegy—Sarah and Freddie the Freeloader

Where are you,
Sarah? Are you
and Freddie, who
watched over town
kids, the town
dump, alone, all
your long lives,
safe?

You were married.
We could never
figure, Freddie—
did you live in
Sarah's house or
in your fumes-of-
burning-plastic
shack?

The heaps of trash
no longer burn, the
never-ending fire
is quenched—the
Feds say it's not
good for the air,
not good for
kids.

But mountain
lions still come
down from the
hills to sniff
scraps. And
there are coyotes,
rats, feral
dogs.

Thirty-five years
on, you must both
be dead. The
professors found new
nannies, housekeepers;
the city pays a
sanitation specialist
now.

II: Legends

Elfego Baca

They thought he was a down-and-dirty
greaser, but he filled them full
of lead. Eighty, a hundred—depends
on who tells it—he held all
at bay.

Five thousand bullets had riddled
the jacal when the lawman
came out.

His compadres rode the miles
to Socorro and back
for the Sheriff, who came
in, got Elfego out, knew
a good man, kept his word.

Blood-Heart Moon

—To Mr. Baca

So hard to
make the way.

The sun wanes,
the moon lifts red.

The washboard road sifts
dust in the tracks.

The stargazer's sight
is spotted, blanched.

Sand whipped his plow-
eyes in youth.

Make the cairn,
make the cairn,
make the cairn
ere the sun rises again.

The Treasure of San Miguel

When men of the uprising
came down the valley, the
friars buried the rail—solid
silver they say—and crossed
the Jornada to old Mexico.

Seek it now, at dark of the
moon, and a phantom
rises, looming above the
sun-white mission, like

Popé urging the people,
village to village, to
drive the pale men in
iron shells down the
river, away from
the sacred places
of home.

San Marcial

Before the waters roiled,
these cement leavings
were railroad shops,
and a future billionaire
was a boy in these streets.

The grand river rose
and took this town—a hundred
years gone. People stop by
on their visits to the Bosque
and the cranes. Green chile

burgers fry at the Owl Bar,
and San Antonio still hangs
on at the Jornada crossroads,
its Anglo railroad-town neighbor
dwindled to concrete walls
and dust.

Flash Flood

U.S. 380 runs ruler-straight
across the malpais, White Sands—
headlights gleam
from twenty miles ahead
some nights.

Dips into arroyos—
no culverts or bridges—
dry-dust reminders
of past rains.

Except in summer,
when thunderheads black-
balloon the sky—
up the arroyo, maybe
miles away.

Then rain rushes down
to fill these gullied dashes
in the blacktop.

It's not good to be first
to pass when these swell,
or to hit the rare night storm,
its roiled black water.

Car swept downstream,
maybe covered by sand
and never found,
the homefolks waiting
in vain.

The Magdalene

When the conquistadores rode
to the high peaks
above a great river
they saw the Magdalene
etched in stone

and knew She willed
a mission nearby, watered,
at the Rio Grande.

Even when Popé came,
took back and killed,
the friars saw She
would guide them away, safe,

and bring them back
in the fullness of His time.

Railroad Corral, Magdalena

Timbers crossed like
giant's lace, smell
of creosote. Last
beeve long gone down
the rusty track. A
leather glove hardens,
loses seams, in the
Nuevo México sun. The
Magdalene rises behind
a downtown brick block
with back doors and trash
barrels facing the corral.

The sour stench of a
thousand travel-crazed,
bawling cattle, the way
their smell got into the
dust on your tongue—that's
an old-timer's story now.
The chute gate, hinges
rusted, is just
hanging on.

Miracle at Laguna

When careful hands
the blessed relic took
into long hiding,
it was as if
a cloud had passed
before our sun,
leaving us heart-struck
but unwillingly tearless.

Now, the centuries-long theft—
however well-intentioned—
is undone.
Morning breaks
over our mesa,
lighting the new day.

San Juan Church[6]

Adobe church stands alone
beside tailing dumps
marking worm-hole mine.

Families returning to their home place,
Saint John's Day, the only supplicants—
most who visit are rockhounds
seeking world-rare smithsonite
in boney-pile gloom.

Common faith in tipple shadow,
built for men who descended
to earth for zinc, copper, silver.

Passing not needle eye
but cage door
as they wound their daily way
except on Sundays.

The Parley with General Sherman, Bosque Redondo

The Great Warrior's mouth
was cruel, but his eyes
looked arrow-straight.

He told us to stand. Outside,
we heard children shout,
cranes calling as they flew
by that wretched spot.

If you can look me in the face,
the Great Warrior said, *then
I know you speak the truth.*

He stood and watched us,
then said, *My children, I
will send you back to
your homes.*

There was something
in his eyes, the smoke
of a thousand burnings. I
could smell the black
cloud, taste the ashes.

And now—I watched, he
sat. The smoke drifted
away, as if a male rain
had finally quenched
the fire.

Captain Mills' Decision

The old chief bled
to death by the
fire.

The little girl clung
to her mother's
torn body.

My troops had
killed the squaw.

I swore to take
the child, to raise
her as my own.

My aide asked how
my wife would like
it, a little Indian girl.

I looked into the
fire, considered it,
thought it best to
leave the child
where I found her.

Lamy

From far-off land the priest came to
beauty: rock, sand and sun.
Where mountain waters trickle down
with endless silver run.

The wooden crucifix is rayed
with spattered drops of blood.
Then vision of a church did rise
in a sudden flood

of faith and love and simple care
for those he'd taken on.
Not a simple man was he but
simpler he'd become.

Zozobra (Old Man Gloom)[7]

Patient giant,
stuffed with all bad virtues—
divorce decree,
positive mammogram,
photo of dead dog.

Doused with inflammable agent,
tickled by match—
festive flare to sky
as crowd gapes.

Fire, heat, smoke, tang
of paper ash
midst autumnal leaf-scent—
and he
is
gone.

From the Cordova Church

A stone is enough to
strike the bell.

Rico gold and silver
give it voice,

form a
cladded cruz.

Sound swells to
the morada,

echoes in the
Sangre de Cristos.

Calls processions of
death, love and penance.

The mule deer in
the meadow
hears, stills, then runs.

Bulto of San Francisco de Asis

Cedar post,
layered fawn and red,

shaped to a dream
of tombed saint,

living now
in wood and thought,

in time far
from his birth.

Pine scent,
dark of night, calls.

The Place of the Fiddle

This is the place.

We judged the cuts
wrong. Enrico's
violin lay far away,
we thought. The tree
crushed her. He ran
to the spot—a
terrible sight. The
head and neck lay
by themselves; her
shattered body hid
under the trunk.

Enrico cried, *She
is gone, she is gone.* The
silent Sangres watched.

He'd saved for
three years to buy
her from Nueva York.

She was a woman.
She moaned like the
night of the moon,
sobbed like a Bataan
widow, or the mother
of a drowned boy.

Jesus, Mary and Joseph.
This is the place.

The Ice Boy's Mother

I want to feel what he felt.

Scolded for thrown knife and fork,
he ran out to winter's dark.
Two days of search, hope, couldn't save him:
snow had covered his tracks.

The first thaw, his daddy found him—
crouched, frozen hard, under a pinyon.
Papers called him the ice boy,
his daddy said—I couldn't read them.

I step outside the cabin.
Scent of pine; stars
sharp pricks in the sky except
where the Sangres block them.

Smoke-smell from the stove fainter
as I pad down the track he took;
ice cuts my bared feet;
wind whips my cotton dress.

But now I'm feeling warmer.

Ranchos de Taos, Noon

Dust-tan-white plaza sprawls
in midday sun.

Package goods window opens
by the mission.

Farmer in ten-gallon grabs
paper sack.

Pickup rumbles
off in dust.

Angelus sounds,
clouds cross the Sangres.

The Death of Fray Ramírez

The garden is
beautiful. Grapes
thrive in

floodplain soil
carried aloft on
women's backs.

A mission crowns
the Sky City.
The campo santo

flourishes with
white-washed
crosses. Their

priest lies
crushed on the
rocks below,

a broken
pitcher at his
feet. Already,

flowers on his
patio wilt.

Now, some say,
when cast from
the rocks, Padre

sprouted wings
and flew, Christ's
martyr, to paradise.

La Llorona of Manuelito

Ghost dancer
leaping, hellfire by
the tracks.

Wailing for the
lost children.

Her man found
them, end of a
day, burnt

dead. Gagged
her, tied her to
the rails.

Now, the cries
along the line,
in the caves, at
the far-away
river, stop blood.

The man, they say,
repented thudding
blows, was
forgiven, is

unbound. The
niños, will-o'-
the-wisp lights,
bob with the
night breeze.

III: Dreaming

By the Palace of the Governors

Children screamed on the plaza as
we stepped inside Woolworth's—
scent of popcorn and floor wax, PVC.

Found Jimmie Rodgers in the bin—
Dad bought it, full price, something
he never did. I near wore it out.

Today, half a country east, I
take Jimmie's accent to heart, speak
it myself when tipsy.

Still play the songs, on CD now,
and wonder if mariachi horns, string
lights, dust still hang on a square
two thousand miles gone.

Miracle

Stair to stars,
rounded, given
with hammer,
saw, square,
bucket of water;

half a world
back, sycamore
gleams white
now that forest
leaves are gone.

The Chief

It's a long way
from Raton,
pass of the rat,
to Arizona.

Rocking these rails,
like metal tire tracks
to the sky.

Signal blades drop,
red.
Dust,
no water,
old adobe,
cart tracks in the sand.
Missions, saloons, cattle.

Albuquerque.
Barrios,
railroad shops,
jewelry tables.

Get off in the heat
while they wash the windows.
Turquoise
twice as much
as in Flagstaff
or Grants.

Here
the Navaho gets on
to tell passengers,
drinking in the lounge,
how Diné words
unwritten,
helped win
the bloody war.

It's getting dark.
We stop
in Gallup.
Littered with mad-dog
bottles
and neon motels.

Where every night
drunken Indians
piss in the park.

To Rudolfo Anaya

Drought-stilled Eno,
silent water.

Bass swims
upriver easily.

Tortuga rests
on a rock.

Now I seek the
Golden Carp

each time
I pass by.

San Esteban del Rey

The crowd shuffled
to cool center
of the adobe church
as a guide told
how all five Ácoma
came back from Bataan.

I looked up at light
flowing into the mission
illuming dust motes
dancing in the seeming-
still air. So many,
all around—and we
    cannot
        usually
           see
                them.

Seeking Jewels[8]

Small showrooms set in adobe
pueblo, smell of pinyon,
cash-only, dark, a novel
experience for the pre-teen,
newly pierced,
fingering handmade
earrings with feathers, turquoise,
silver filigree.

Outside, clear, cold creek,
spanned by four bridges,
calls her little brother,
who's crossing back and forth,
back and forth, above
bright, wet rocks like gems,
in sun shadowed by high
walls, blue mountains.

Zuni Event Day

Typical dusty summer weekday,
pull up at the pumps.

Lights on in the station,
everything seems as always.

But the pumps won't turn on.

Inside, staff cleaning, painting:
Sorry, we're closed.

Nearest gas, *Seventy miles ahead
or backtrack twenty.*

We turn around, fill up at service
station/package goods store

just off the rez. The lady
at checkout gives the kids

candy. She's friendly, festive.
These are special days.

Stickmen at Chaco

Figures incised stone on stone,
the petroglyphs face me, my son,
when we reach the cliff.

Like the "Stickman Odyssey",
my son says. I recall Dr. Watson, speaking
of Neolithic man emerging

from his Dartmoor hut. Dry summer
heat surrounds us, not a wisp
of wind. Archeologist-advised
guidebook gives mere guesses

of meaning, as ancient runes stand
in still lines all around us,
on outcrops facing the dying,
western sun.

Playtime

Desert dervish pushes, the teeter-
totter creaks. Off the path,
there's cactus spine, rattlesnake
strike, centipede sting.

Wild gourd slithers by the slide,
goathead plants creep along
the field. A raven lands
by the jungle-gym, croak-calls

but there is no one to drop
pepitas, biscochitos. A gust
sidewinds across the playground,
whips up a dust devil,

coiling opaque in full sun. Swing
grates on rusty chain,
but its riders, grown or gone,
do not return.

Prophecy

—September 9, 2001

These seem
the best days,

the water clear,
just chilling.

Rippled by minnows.

Above the stream,
mountains march
in a line like giants.

At the tree line,
what stirs,

what black
shape rises

to scatter
sunning cougars,

to rout even
the old ones,
watching over the people,
from ancient hills?

Seek the cars, the
houses, the
rising dust
behind your wheels—

it does not suffice.

Glossary:

acequia: small irrigation ditch, usually overseen by an official called a mayordomo

Ácoma: the Sky City, a pueblo in western New Mexico

arroyo: small canyon; gulch

barrios: neighborhoods

biscochitos: traditional New Mexican cookie associated with weddings and Christmas

bosque: forest; in the Socorro, N.M. area, Bosque (capitalized) generally refers to Bosque del Apache, a nearby National Wildlife Refuge

Bosque Redondo: A reservation near Fort Sumner, N.M. to which the Navaho (Navajo, Diné) and Mescalero Apache tribes were forcibly moved for a number of years during the Civil War period; in a chilling parallel with the Cherokee "Trail of Tears" in the eastern U.S., the Navaho call this removal "The Long Walk"

burro: donkey

campo santo: graveyard

compadres: pals, buddies

cruz: cross

curandera: folk healer, herbal healer (female)

diablo: devil

Diné: the Navaho (also spelled Navajo) people in their own language; literally, "the people"

establo: stable

jacal: an adobe style housing structure historically found throughout parts of the southwestern United States and Mexico

Jornada del Muerto: a waterless area between Las Cruces and Socorro, N.M.; literally, "journey of the dead man"

La Llorona: "the Weeping Woman," a tragic and dangerous spirit who killed her own children and then committed suicide; has similarities to the Celtic banshee; is condemned to wander forever; usually found along rivers, since she killed her children by drowning them

luminaria: traditionally, small bonfire lighting the way for the holy family on Christmas Eve; in modern times, a farolito, a candle in a bag weighted by sand, is often called a luminaria; in the eastern U.S., where they have recently become popular, often called a "luminary"

malpais: badlands, usually a former lava flow area

misa: mass (Catholic)

morada: Penitente house of worship or brotherhood house; the Penitentes, "Los Hermanos Penitentes", is a Catholic religious brotherhood found largely in northern New Mexico

Noche Buena (or Nochebuena): Christmas Eve

osha or oshá: medicinal herb, *Ligusticum porteri*

padre: (Catholic) priest

pepitas: roasted pumpkin seeds

Popé (or Po'pay): Native American who led the Pueblo Revolt of 1680 in New Mexico

Posadas (Las Posadas): nine-day Christmas celebration beginning December 16 and ending on Christmas Day; Spanish in origin; literally, "the inns," from the Bible story of Jesus' birth

rico: rich; wealthy people

San Esteban del Rey: Saint Stephen the King, Catholic saint, patron of the country of Hungary; church in Ácoma named for this saint

San Felipé de Neri (church): large Catholic church in the Old Town section of Albuquerque, N.M.; named for King Philip of Spain

San Francisco de Asis: Saint Francis of Assisi, Catholic saint, patron of animals and the environment

San Miguel (Mission): Catholic church in Socorro, N.M., named for Saint Michael, the Archangel

Sangre de Cristos (also, Sangres): a range of mountains in northern New Mexico and southern Colorado; literally, "blood of Christ," so-called from the beautiful colors they show

stargazer: Navaho medicine man, mystic, healer, diviner

tortuga: turtle

yerbas: herbs

Note: The poet has used spellings—such as pinyon, Navaho, luminaria for a farolito—that were current among Caucasian New Mexicans during his childhood. Navajo and piñon, for example, are more correct usages.

Notes

1 *With tonight being Christmas Eve magical things can occur—one of which is the folklore belief that animals can speak. Anyone still possessing a barn that contains farm animals can—if they're very quiet and careful—sneak up to it at midnight and hear their livestock discussing their master; just as the animals in the stable on that first Christmas night discussed the arrival of the Great Master.* —"The Waterman and Hill-Traveller's Companion, a Natural Events Almanac."

2 In one of the most famous UFO sightings, policeman Lonnie Zamora saw a strange oval-shaped object near Socorro, New Mexico in 1964.

3 Also Saint Patrick's Day.

4 A children's show on KGGM-TV, Albuquerque.

5 The Kelly Mine yielded lead, copper, zinc and silver. Ore was treated at the Billing Smelter in Socorro, then the Graphic Smelter in Magdalena.

6 At Kelly, NM, a ghost town.

7 Zozobra ("Old Man Gloom") is a giant effigy who is burned every fall during the Santa Fe (New Mexico) fiesta. Although Zozobra seems like an ancient folklore manifestation of the fiesta, which was founded in 1712, he was actually created by artist William Howard "Will" Shuster, Jr., in 1924.

8 Taos, New Mexico, Summer 2011.

Senior associate director of the Institute for the Environment at the University of North Carolina at Chapel Hill, Tony Reevy is a graduate of North Carolina State University, UNC-Chapel Hill and Miami University. He is a David P. Morgan Award winner (2006) and a Pushcart Prize nominee. His previous publications include poetry, non-fiction and short fiction, including the non-fiction books *Ghost Train!*, *O. Winston Link: Life Along the Line* and *The Railroad Photography of Jack Delano*; the full books of poetry, *Old North* and *Passage*; and the poetry chapbooks *Green Cove Stop, Magdalena, Lightning in Wartime*, and *In Mountain Lion Country*. Reevy spent much of his childhood in Socorro, New Mexico. He resides in Durham, North Carolina with wife, Caroline Weaver, and children Lindley and Ian.

www.ingramcontent.com/pod-product-compliance
Lightning Source LLC
Chambersburg PA
CBHW022118090426
42743CB00008B/904